Native Americans

Seminole Indians

Caryn Yacowitz

Heinemann Library
Chicago, Illinois

©2003 Heinemann Library
a division of Reed Elsevier Inc.
Chicago, Illinois

Customer Service 888-454-2279

Visit our website at www.heinemannlibrary.com

Photo research by Alan Gottlieb
Printed and bound in the United States by Lake Book Manufacturing, Inc.

07 06 05 04 03
10 9 8 7 6 5 4 3 2 1

Library of Congress Cataloging-in-Publication Data
Yacowitz, Caryn.
  Seminole Indians / Caryn Yacowitz.
     v. cm. -- (Native Americans)
Includes bibliographical references and index.
Contents: Land of sun and swamp -- The first Seminole -- Hunting,
fishing, and farming -- Families and clans -- Chickees and dugouts --
Colorful clothing -- Seminole games -- Medicine, religion, and spirits
-- A Seminole story -- The Green Corn Ceremony -- The Seminole are
divided -- Brave leaders -- Oklahoma and Florida Seminole today -- The
Seminole adapt and survive.
  ISBN 1-40340-304-X (lib. bdg.) -- ISBN 1-40340-511-5 (pbk.)
  1. Seminole Indians--Juvenile literature. [1. Seminole Indians. 2.
Indians of North America--Southern States.] I. Title. II. Native
Americans (Heinemann Library (Firm))
  E99.S28 Y33 2002
  975.004'973--dc21
                                        2002006324

Acknowledgments
The author and publisher are grateful to the following for permission to reproduce copyright material: pp. 4, 5 David Muench/Corbis;
p. 7 courtesy William Loren Katz Collection; p. 8 Galen Rowell/Corbis; pp. 9, 24 Library of Congress; pp. 10, 12, 13, 14, 15, 26 Florida
State Archives; p. 11 National Museum of American Art, Washington, D.C./Art Resource p. 16 Seminole Nation Museum; pp. 17, 18,
23B, 29 Marilyn "Angel" Wynn/Nativestock; pp. 19, 28, 30 Communications Department Photographers/Seminole Tribe of Florida;
p. 20 David and Hayes Norris/Photo Researchers, Inc.; p. 21 Noah Billie/Courtesy Seminole Tribe of Florida; p. 22 Drawing by Willie
Lena/Seminole Nation Museum; p. 23T Bettmann/Corbis; p. 25 North Wind Picture Archive; p. 27 National Portrait Gallery,
Smithsonian Institution/Art Resource.

Cover photograph by National Museum of American Art, Washington, D.C./Art Resource.

Special thanks to Pare Bowlegs for his help in the preparation of this book.

Some words are shown in bold, **like this.** You can find out
what they mean by looking in the glossary.

Contents

Land of Sun and Swamp

A piece of land stretches into the sea in the southeast part of the United States. Today, this is the state of Florida. The Atlantic Ocean and the warm **Gulf** of Mexico surround Florida on three sides. It is a land of hot summers and mild, rainy winters.

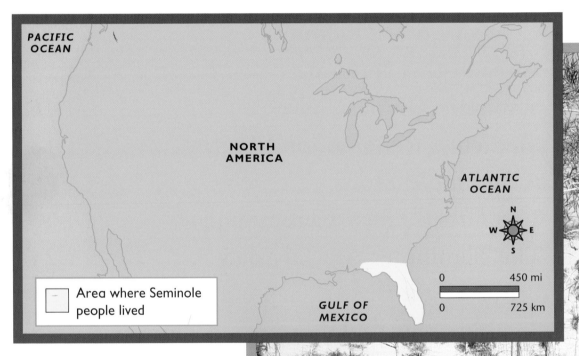

PACIFIC OCEAN

NORTH AMERICA

ATLANTIC OCEAN

N
W E
S

Area where Seminole people lived

GULF OF MEXICO

0   450 mi
0   725 km

Rolling hills of rich, red clay soil are found in the northern part of Florida. Thick forests of pine and other trees once grew here. Large **swamps** with **cypress, mangrove,** and **palm** trees are found in the south. Native people call these wet grasslands "the river of grass." Many kinds of birds and animals live in the swamps, including alligators and **manatees.**

The First Seminoles

The Seminoles are a young **tribe.** The tribe was created about 300 years ago, in the early 1700s. Groups of Creek Indians

The Seminole Name

People began to call the Freedmen and Indians "Seminoles." The name *Seminole* comes from a Spanish word meaning "wild."

from what are now the states of Georgia and Alabama came to Florida. Later **slaves** came as well. The slaves had escaped from **plantations.** The escaped slaves were called Freedmen. The Freedmen and the Indians lived together. They got along well.

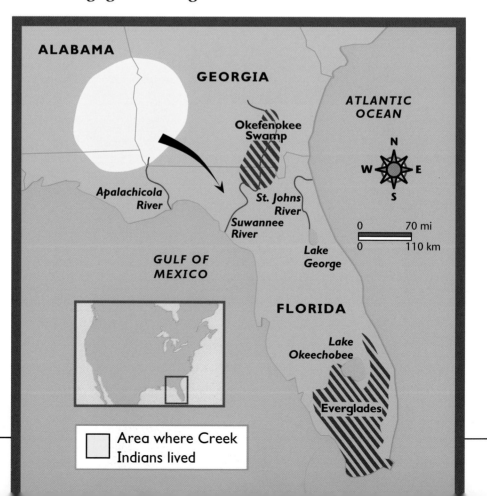

Area where Creek Indians lived

6

The Seminoles went to Florida because they wanted freedom, good farmland, and animals to hunt. They also went to get away from the battles among the white **settlers** north of Florida.

Escaped slaves went to Florida to be free.

Hunting, Fishing, and Farming

The Seminoles fished and hunted deer, bears, and other animals. The land in northern Florida was good for growing corn, pumpkins, beans, squash, and melons. They also raised cattle and horses. Later, white **settlers** from the north wanted this land for themselves. They forced the Seminoles out of northern Florida. The Seminoles went to the Everglades, a **swampy** part of southern Florida.

The swamps were full of plants and animals. The Seminoles used some plants for food and others for medicine.

These Seminole women are grinding corn to make sofkee.

The swamps were not good for farming. Seminoles found **hummocks** where they could grow corn, sweet potatoes, and pumpkins. They drank *sofkee,* a drink made from crushed corn boiled in water. They ate *coontie,* a pudding made from arrow plant roots. As the seasons changed, Seminoles hunted animals in the swamps for food and **pelts.** They hunted raccoons, deer, rabbits, alligators, snakes, and turtles. Seminoles ate alligator meat, but they never ate snake. They caught many kinds of fish.

Families and Clans

Families who were related to one another lived in groups called **clans.** Every clan had a special name. Some clan names were Wind, Panther, Deer, Bird, Alligator, Beaver, and Bear. When people married, they had to choose someone from a different clan. The children became part of the mother's clan. For example, if a Panther clan woman married a Bird clan man, their children would be part of the Panther clan.

Seminole children are part of their mother's clan.

Seminole boys were taught to hunt with bows and arrows.

Each clan took care of its members and taught the children. Boys learned hunting and fishing from their fathers and their uncles. Mothers taught their daughters to farm, **weave** baskets, sew, and make **pottery.** During the year, clans gathered to celebrate **religious festivals** and marriages.

Chickees and Dugouts

The first Seminoles built log houses like the Creek Indians. Every family had two houses. One house was for sleeping and cooking. The other house was used for storing **belongings** and for visitors. In the 1800s, white **settlers** forced the Seminoles to move to the **swamps**. Seminoles built a different kind of house there.

A chickee has open sides to let the breeze through. This keeps chickees cool.

Seminole canoes moved quickly and quietly. The flat bottoms helped them float smoothly over the water.

In the swamps, Seminoles built *chickees*. *Chickees* were raised above the mud and water. The roof was made of **palmetto** leaves. The sides were open to let cool breezes blow through. Every family had a *chickee* for sleeping and storing belongings. Cooking for the whole village was done in one *chickee*.

Travel in the Everglades

The Seminoles used streams in the Everglades to travel through the "river of grass." Seminoles made strong, light canoes from **cypress** logs. They used poles to push the canoes through the shallow water.

13

Patchwork Clothing

In the early 1700s, the Seminoles wore **buckskin** clothes. Later, they traded with British and Spanish **settlers** for cotton cloth. The women made long skirts and blouses. They wore short **shawls** around their shoulders. Men wore long cotton shirts. They wore cloth hats called **turbans.**

These Seminole men are wearing turbans and cotton shirts.

*These Seminole girls are wearing **traditional** patchwork clothing and bead necklaces.*

Around 1918, Seminoles started using sewing machines. They decorated their clothing with bands of colored cloth. The Seminoles became famous for their beautiful **patchwork** designs. Some Seminole women wore many necklaces. Each year, a girl received more of them. By the time she was grown up, her neck and shoulders were covered with many necklaces.

Seminole Games

Today, Seminole men play stickball. Long ago, they played the game as part of **religious ceremonies**. Sometimes it was used to end an argument between groups of people. Men played using two long rackets made of wood. Each racket had a small cup at the end. The ball was made of deerskin. Stickball was a very rough game. Players often broke an arm or leg. "Little Brother of War" is the Seminole nickname for stickball.

These Seminole men are playing stickball on tribal land in Oklahoma. The photograph was taken in the early 1900s.

*Today, Seminole men and women enjoy playing **lacrosse**. It is like the Indian stickball game of long ago.*

When women played the ball game with men, they did not use rackets. This game was not as rough. Men and women also played a game with a small, round wooden disk. They threw **spears** at the disk as it rolled like a tire.

Medicine, Religion, and Spirits

Medicine is part of Seminole **religion**. Seminoles believe a person's body and **spirit** are the same. If someone is sick, a medicine man or medicine woman helps them get well. They use special plants and roots that are kept in a medicine bundle. The medicine bundle is **sacred**.

*This Seminole medicine man is performing a **ceremony** called the Rainmaker Dance.*

18

The Milky Way is a bright band of stars in the night sky.
Seminoles believe the Milky Way was created by Master of Breath.

Seminoles call the creator of the world Master of Breath. Master of Breath made all the animals, taught people to fish, gave them the pumpkin plant, and made the **Milky Way**. Seminoles believe that all living things—plants, animals, and people—are connected. They say prayers before killing an animal for food. Many Seminoles still follow these beliefs and **customs**.

A Seminole Story

The Seminoles tell a story about how plants and animals came to Earth. First, Master of Breath made all the animals and plants. Then he put them into a shell. He set the shell on the ground. A tree root cracked the shell and Wind came out. Then came the first animal, Panther. Next came Deer, Bird, Alligator, Beaver, and Bear.

Some panthers still live in the Everglades. Today, some members of the Seminole Panther clan become lawyers.

This painting by Seminole artist Noah Billie shows children learning about how the clans were formed.

Master of Breath put the animals into **clans** and gave them powers. Panther would make laws. Bird would make sure things were in the right place. Bear kept the fire. Wind, which lets all creatures breathe, would help everyone. Each animal had certain powers and a special place on the earth.

The Green Corn Ceremony

The most important Seminole **festival** is the Green Corn **Ceremony.** In July or August, Seminoles celebrate the first sweet corn. The medicine man adds new plants to the medicine bundle to keep the **tribe** powerful. Many people get married at this time. Boys who turn fifteen get their second name and become adult members of the tribe. Long ago, crimes were judged during the Green Corn Ceremony.

Women perform the Ribbon Dance at the Green Corn Ceremony.

Many Seminole couples get married during the Green Corn Ceremony.

Everyone sings and performs **religious** dances. Women dance the Ribbon Dance. Men dance the Feather Dance. In the Stomp Dance, women called shell-shakers keep the beat. Shell-shakers wear leg rattles. These are made of turtle shells filled with small stones. It is a happy time. All of the fires are put out. Then a medicine man lights the fires again so a new year can begin.

The Seminoles Are Divided

When the Seminoles came to Florida, some Spanish **settlers** were already there. They lived near one another in peace. In 1817, the United States fought a war with the Spanish for control of Florida. Florida became part of the United States in 1821. Settlers from the United States wanted Seminole land. **Plantation** owners from southern states wanted their **slaves** back. Soldiers forced the Seminoles into central and southern Florida.

Seminole warriors attacked United States government forts that had been built on Seminole land.

This painting shows United States soldiers capturing Seminole chiefs during the First Seminole War.

In 1835, Andrew Jackson was president of the United States. He wanted Indian lands for white settlers, so he signed a law. It forced the Seminoles and other **tribes** to go to the Indian Territory in present-day Oklahoma. More than 3,000 Seminoles left Florida between 1836 and 1859. One of every three Seminoles died during the trip. Only 200 Seminoles were left in Florida. They hid in the Everglades and fought to **protect** their land. The Seminole Wars lasted for more than 40 years.

Brave Leaders

The most famous war leader of the Seminoles was Osceola. He wanted his people to be free. Osceola would not sign the **treaty** forcing the Seminoles to leave Florida. Many Seminoles say he stuck his knife into the treaty. Osceola led his warriors into battle against the United States Army. He went to talk with the army's general. Osceola was carrying a white flag of peace. But the general did not pay attention to the peace flag. He put Osceola in prison, where he died three months later.

This painting shows Osceola refusing the treaty offered by the United States government.

Chief Billy Bowlegs fought to keep control of Seminole lands in present-day Florida.

Other Seminole leaders like Wildcat, Alligator, and Chief Billy Bowlegs also helped their people. The Seminoles can proudly call themselves the only **undefeated tribe** in the United States.

Seminoles in Oklahoma and Florida

Today, Seminoles live in Oklahoma and Florida. There are about 12,000 Seminoles in Oklahoma. They are farmers, teachers, doctors, and artists. Most still celebrate the Green Corn **Ceremony**. Children learn the Seminole language, Muscogee. They also learn Seminole dances and songs.

Big Cypress Reservation

Most of the 3,000 Seminoles in Florida make their homes on five **reservations**. The largest is the Big **Cypress** Reservation. It covers over 42,000 acres in the Everglades.

*These Seminole children are at a tribal fair. They are dressed in **traditional patchwork** clothing.*

28

This Seminole man is helping to build an airplane.

The Seminoles who live in Florida also work in many different jobs. They are cattle ranchers, farmers, construction workers, nurses, doctors, and teachers. Some speak the Muscogee language, but most speak Hetchete. Hetchete is another Seminole language. Like their relatives in Oklahoma, Florida Seminoles celebrate the Green Corn Ceremony.

The Seminoles Today

In both Oklahoma and Florida, Seminoles still know their **clan**. Seminole leaders in Oklahoma think that teaching children the Seminole languages is a very important way of continuing the Seminole way of life. The Seminole people have had to change the way they live in order to survive. As a Seminole **elder** said, "The fire of our people is still burning." The Seminoles are strong and proud. They are **undefeated**.

*Betty Mae Tiger Jumper keeps Seminole **traditions** strong by telling stories.*

Glossary

belonging   something a person owns

buckskin   deerskin leather made soft by tanning

ceremony   event that celebrates a special occasion

clan   group of families that are related

custom   something that has been done for a long time

cypress   evergreen tree with small, dark green leaves

elder   older person

festival   day or time of celebration

gulf   large area of ocean that reaches into land

hummock   low hill

lacrosse   ball game played today with long-handled wooden rackets

manatee   large plant-eating animal with a flat tail and flippers

mangrove   tropical tree that sends down many roots

Milky Way   band of stars stretching across the night sky

palm   tree with a tall, thin trunk and a bunch of large leaves at the top

palmetto   small palm tree with leaves shaped like a fan

patchwork   type of sewing in which pieces of different-colored cloth are sewn together

pelt   animal skin with fur

plantation   large farm. People who worked there were often slaves.

pottery   pots, dishes, and other things made of clay

protect   keep from harm or danger

religion   system of spiritual beliefs and practices

reservation   land kept by Indians when they signed treaties

sacred   holy; something that has special meaning for a community or tribe

settler   person who makes a home in a new place

shawl   large piece of cloth worn over the shoulders

slave   person who was bought and sold as a worker

spear   long, straight weapon with a sharp blade at one end

spirit   invisible force or being with special power

swamp   wet, spongy land

tradition   custom or story that has been passed from older people to younger people for a long time

treaty   agreement between governments or groups of people

tribe   group of people who share language, customs, beliefs, and often government

turban   long scarf wound around the head many times

undefeated   never lost a battle

weave   lace together threads or other material

More Books to Read

Ansary, Mir Tanim. *Southeast Indians*. Chicago: Heinemann Library, 1999.

Petra Press Staff. *The Seminole*. Minneapolis: Compass Point Books, 2001.

Sonneborn, Liz. *The Seminole: Indians of the Americas*. Danbury, Conn.: Scholastic Library Publishing, 2002.

Wickman, Patricia R. *Seminole Colors: A Coloring and Learning Book for Young Minds*. Hollywood, Fla.: Seminole Tribe of Florida, Department of Anthropology & Genealogy, 1999.

Index